SERVING WITH POLICE, FIRE & EMS

OPPORTUNITIES TO VOLUNTEER

by Bernard Ryan, Jr.

Ryan, Bernard, 1923-
    Community service for teens: opportunities to volunteer / Bernard
Ryan, Jr.
        p. cm.
    Includes bibliographical references and index.
    Contents: [1] Caring for animals -- [2] Expanding education and
literacy -- [3] Helping the ill, the poor & the elderly -- [4] Increasing
neighborhood service -- [5] Participating in government --
- -[6] Promoting the arts and sciences -- [7] Protecting the environment
- -[8] Serving with police, fire & EMS
    ISBN 0-89434-227-4 (v. 1). -- ISBN 0-89434-231-2 (v. 2). -- ISBN
0-89434-229-0 (v. 3). -- ISBN 0-89434-233-9 (v. 4). --
ISBN 0-89434-230-4 (v. 5). -- ISBN 0-89434-234-7 (v. 6). --
ISBN 0-89434-228-2 (v. 7). -- ISBN 0-89434-232-0 (v. 8)
    1. Voluntarism—United States—Juvenile literature. 2. Young
volunteers—United States—Juvenile literature. 3. Teenage
volunteers in social service—United States—Juvenile literature.
[1. Voluntarism.] I. Title.
HN90.V64R93   1998
361.3'7'o8350973—dc21   97-34971
                                                              CIP
                                                              AC

Community Service for Teens: Serving with Police, Fire & EMS:
Opportunities to Volunteer

A New England Publishing Associates Book
Copyright ©1998 by Ferguson Publishing Company
ISBN 0-89434-232-0

Published and distributed by
Ferguson Publishing Company
200 West Madison, Suite 300
Chicago, Illinois 60606
800-306-9941
Web Site: http://www.fergpubco.com

Printed in the United States of America
V-3

CONTENTS

High school junior Jenn Lonegan is an active member of Southbury, Connecticut, Police Explorer Post 130.

(Bernard Ryan, Jr.)

INTRODUCTION

WHO VOLUNTEERS?

Six out of ten American teenagers work as volunteers. A 1996 survey revealed that the total number of teen volunteers aged 12 to 17 is 13.3 million. They give 2.4 billion hours each year. Of that time, 1.8 billion hours are spent in "formal" commitments to nonprofit organizations. Informal help, like "just helping neighbors," receives 600 million hours.

Each "formal" volunteer gives an average of three and a half hours a week. It would take nearly 1.1 million full-time employees to match these hours. And if the formal volunteers were paid minimum wage for their time, the cost would come to at least $7.7 billion—a tremendous saving to nonprofit organizations.

Teen volunteerism is growing. In the four years between the 1996 survey and a previous one, the number of volunteers grew by 7 percent and their hours increased by 17 percent.

Equal numbers of girls and boys give their time to volunteering.

How voluntary is volunteering? Only 16 out of 100 volunteers go to schools that insist on community service before graduation. Twenty-six out of 100 are in schools that offer courses requiring community service to get credit for the course.

Six out of ten teen volunteers started volunteering before they were 14 years old. Seventy-eight percent of teens who volunteer have parents who volunteer.

WHY VOLUNTEER?

Only 16 out of 100 volunteers go to schools that insist on community service before graduation.

When teens are asked to volunteer, the 1996 survey revealed, nine out of ten do so. Who does the asking? Usually it's a friend, teacher, family member, relative or church member.

Teens gave a number of reasons for volunteering, regardless of whether their schools required community service. Their reasons included:

- You feel compassion for people in need.
- You feel you can do something for a cause that is important to you.
- You believe that if you help others, others will help you.
- Your volunteering is important to people you respect.
- You learn to relate to others who may be different from you.
- You develop leadership skills.
- You become more patient.
- You gain a better understanding of good citizenship.
- You get a chance to learn about various careers.
- You gain experience that can help in school and can lead to college admission and college scholarships as well as future careers.

VOLUNTEER FOR WHAT?

You can volunteer in a wide variety of activities. To get a picture of how teen volunteering is spread among various categories, see Exhibit 1.

CRISIS OR NEAR-CRISIS SITUATIONS

In Exhibit 1, note three sections: human services, 7.1 percent; health, 6.5 percent; and public/societal benefit, 3.7 percent. These add up to 17.3 percent of

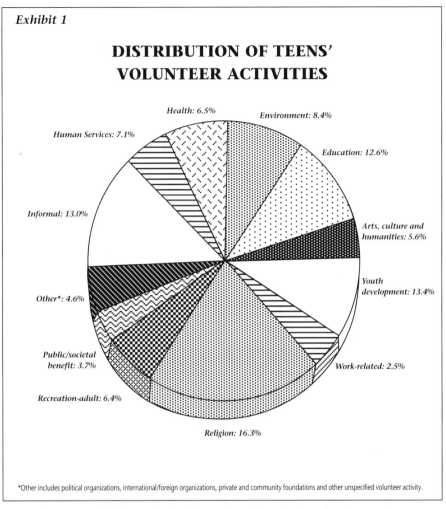

Exhibit 1

DISTRIBUTION OF TEENS' VOLUNTEER ACTIVITIES

Health: 6.5%

Environment: 8.4%

Human Services: 7.1%

Education: 12.6%

Informal: 13.0%

Arts, culture and humanities: 5.6%

Youth development: 13.4%

Other*: 4.6%

Public/societal benefit: 3.7%

Work-related: 2.5%

Recreation-adult: 6.4%

Religion: 16.3%

*Other includes political organizations, international/foreign organizations, private and community foundations and other unspecified volunteer activity.

(Source: Volunteering and Giving Among American Teenagers: 1996. Independent Sector, Washington, D.C., 1997.)

all the volunteer activities studied. That's almost 20 percent, or one out of every five teen volunteers. The subjects you will read about in this book fall into these three areas. They involve serving, or being ready to serve, in crisis or near-crisis situations.

The following pages are divided into three areas of volunteerism: police department, volunteer fire department and emergency medical service (EMS) work. In addition, some other areas, such as the Civil Air Patrol (CAP), are covered.

WHO SAYS YOU HAVE TO "VOLUNTEER"?

Is "volunteering" for community service required in your school? It is if you live in the state of Maryland or in the city of Atlanta, Georgia. In fact, in many school districts across the United States you cannot receive your high school diploma unless you have spent a certain number of hours in community service. The number of hours varies.

Who makes the rule? In Maryland, the only state so far to require every high school student to perform community service, it is the Maryland State Department of Education. In most school districts, it is the board of education, which usually sets policies that meet the standards of the community.

If you have to do it, is it voluntary? And is it legal to *make* you do it? One family didn't think so. In 1994, the parents of Daniel Immediato, a 17-year-old senior at Rye Neck High School in Mamaroneck, New York, sued in federal court to keep Daniel's school from requiring him to spend 40 hours in community service before he could graduate.

Daniel's parents said the requirement interfered with their right to raise their child, that it violated Daniel's privacy rights, and that it was a violation of the Thirteenth Amendment to the U.S. Constitution. That amendment says:

> Neither slavery nor involuntary servitude, except as a punishment for a crime whereof the party shall have been duly convicted, shall exist within the United States, or any place subject to their jurisdiction.

The requirement for community service, said the Immediatos, imposed involuntary servitude on Daniel.

In its defense, the Rye Neck School Board argued that what it wanted was to get the students out into the community to see what goes on in the outside world. In the process, said the board, students would find out what it was like to have to dress appropriately for a job, be on time somewhere and have other people dependent on them. The emphasis was not on what the community would gain; it was on what the student would learn.

The court decided the school system was right. The Immediatos appealed. The U.S. Court of Appeals for the Second Circuit upheld the decision. The Immediatos asked the Supreme Court of the United States to hear the case. It turned down the request, as it does many appeals, without stating its reason for refusing.

PART ONE
Volunteer Police Work

CHAPTER ONE
Police Explorers

*I*n nearly 3,000 cities and towns across America, some 46,000 teenage volunteers serve their communities as members of Law Enforcement Explorer Posts in police departments. Any one post may have as few as 3 to 4 teens or as many as 20 to 60. If you divide 46,000 by 3,000, you will see that the average post has 15 members.

Each Explorer Post has at least one police officer assigned to it as the post adviser.

Why are teen volunteers in police departments called "explorers"? Because the program originally grew out of the Explorer Division of the Boy Scouts of America. To be a Police Explorer today, however, you do not have to be a Boy Scout, nor do you have to be a boy.

EXPLORER POST ADVISER

Each Explorer Post has at least one police officer assigned to it as the post adviser. This officer is responsible for selecting teens to join the post. He or she works hard to maintain training, supervise assignments and judge how the post members are doing.

The organization is run by the members themselves. As a member, you join in electing a president, vice president, secretary, and treasurer from among your peers. Your post adviser appoints—from among the teen explorers—the post's chief, deputy chief, lieutenant, sergeant and quartermaster.

YOUR QUALIFICATIONS

To get into an Explorer Post, you must be at least 14 years old and a student in high school. You are allowed to stay in the post until you turn 21. Your parents or guardians must give their approval by signing a general liability release form. You have to be in good health, with good moral habits and no record of arrest or conviction on any serious offense. And you must maintain satisfactory grades in school.

Before the post accepts you, one or more of the post advisers—police officers or civilians who work with them—interview you and investigate your background. When you are admitted, you begin a six-month probationary period. During this time, you go through a basic training program and evaluation process.

Don't worry about bringing special skills with you to the Police Explorers. You don't need any. What they are looking for is your interest. They want you to be there once every week for the meeting and training session. And they want you to be on call for emergencies and special-duty assignments. Most police departments have plenty of both for their explorers to work at.

We teach you everything. If you don't know a Band-Aid from an Ace bandage, that's not a problem. When you leave here, you'll know.

—Officer Matthew McNally,
Police Explorers Adviser,
Danbury, Connecticut

CHAPTER TWO

What You'll Do as a Police Explorer

As a Police Explorer, your duties will cover a wide variety of work that is routine in police departments. Some is planned, so you know well ahead of time just what you will be doing. Some is not planned. Rather, it is spur-of-the-moment when a particular need arises, like searching for people, searching for criminal evidence, performing crowd and traffic control or providing security services.

SEARCH FOR PEOPLE

Suppose a frantic mother calls the police. "I can't find my three-year-old," she says. "She's wandered away from the house." The officer on duty immediately calls the chief of your Police Explorer Post. The chief calls the deputies, who call their sergeants. A squad of explorers, most of whom are 16 or older and have driver's licenses, goes quickly to police headquarters. If you do not have a license or a car, you are picked up by an explorer who does.

At headquarters, the officer has made copies of a map of the neighborhood to be searched and has marked it with grid lines. This gives each of you a specific area to search.

Whether the missing person is a small child or an elderly grandparent, the same system is used. As they conduct the search, explorers save the time and energy of many other police officers. In fact, most police departments lack the personnel to send 20 or 30 officers out looking for a missing person. So the Police Explorer system saves the local government money.

SEARCH FOR CRIMINAL EVIDENCE

Missing people are not the only subjects of searches. A gun, a knife, a stolen wallet or purse may be tossed somewhere by a criminal rushing from a crime scene.

Witnesses, no two of whom are ever sure to agree, say something was thrown from a moving car, down an embankment, into a gully—wherever.

Police officers who are "evidence technicians" ask the Police Explorer Post to help search for the missing evidence. This time, you may be down on your hands and knees, looking through soggy underbrush. Or you may join a line of 15 or 20 explorers moving abreast through a park or across an open field or along the edge of a highway. You search carefully, because you know homicides and lesser crimes have been solved by tiny bits of evidence found by Police Explorers.

Our explorers have helped solve two homicides since I've been in charge. We probably would have had a hard time getting convictions on the arrests, because we were missing bits of information. I get them looking for the most microscopic stuff out there.

—Officer Matthew McNally

CROWD AND TRAFFIC CONTROL

Wherever crowds gather, police need help to guide people on foot, on bikes or in-line skates or in cars, trucks and campers.

Indoors, you may help direct pedestrian traffic at crowded crafts fairs, exhibitions and concerts. Outdoors, at Fourth of July fireworks, carnivals, circuses, fairs, parades and walkathons, you may be in charge of controlling heavy traffic. This means that, as cop talk puts it, "You supply crosswalk detail." You stop traffic as runners come by. You run to get first aid or call the EMS if someone falls or is injured.

The event may be unplanned. You may be called suddenly to help control traffic at a major fire or accident scene. But whether it is a planned event or one that just happened, your training will help you understand how crowds behave. You will apply your judgment to whether this line of people or cars has stood still so long that it must be given its turn to move. And you will apply large amounts of your own patience to meet the impatience of the public.

SECURITY

At some events, you may act as a guard or security person. Antiques shows and crafts fairs, for example, need people in uniform to keep an eye on items that are for sale and to watch for shoplifting or other theft. Another example: At a county- or statewide Boy Scout jamboree, your Explorer Post may serve on security duty 24 hours a day. One of the things you learn about your uniform is that most people respect it and, in fact, usually don't notice that you are a teenager. They may think, "My, that's a young-looking police officer," but few are critical.

Many organizations use explorers at charitable and social events. Police Explorer Bill Silva notes that the group provides *cost-effective* security and crowd and traffic control.

"Your organization doesn't have to pay any money," reports Silva. "We provide a great service. If you're holding a charitable event, the last thing you want to do is spend $40 an hour to have cops there when you can have 20 of us there to do the job. Maybe you buy us some pizza, if you're nice. We direct traffic, we hold the crowds back and do security sometimes. Our main focus is on parades and non-profit events."

CHAPTER THREE

What Does It Take to Be a Police Explorer?

*A*s a Police Explorer, you will be required to attend weekly meetings, maintain physical and mental discipline, be responsible for your uniform and equipment as well as meet particular attitude and scholastic requirements.

REGULAR ATTENDANCE

As part of your duty, you attend a training session one evening every week. Often a guest speaker describes some specific area of police work. Some training sessions are held "in the field"—at a heavy-traffic location or a mock crime scene, for example.

Regular-duty assignments are usually scheduled for weekends and during school breaks and summer vacations. Emergency assignments such as a search, of course, come without warning.

Does being a Police Explorer mean you have no time for anything else? No. You can schedule your explorer time around school and family events—sports, clubs, whatever. The important thing is to be there when you are supposed to be there—promptly and willingly—especially at the weekly training sessions.

Regular-duty assignments are usually scheduled for weekends and during school breaks and summer vacations.

PHYSICAL AND MENTAL DISCIPLINE

Some of the basic physical discipline is very much like military drills. You line up. You stand at attention. You march. You do basic exercises to help build up your strength. You do push-ups. Why push-ups? Because when you go to the shooting range, you will need plenty of strength in your upper body.

Mental discipline involves learning to take orders and follow a chain of command headed by the post adviser. You learn organization.

Certain Police Explorer jobs, to which you may be elected one day, give you

(Bernard Ryan, Jr.)

*High school senior Dan Cohn has volunteered in Law
Enforcement Exploring Post 33, Danbury, Connecticut,
since the summer between seventh and eighth grades.*

special responsibilities. The president runs all meetings. The vice president handles recruiting new members and administering the post's program. The secretary keeps the records. The treasurer is in charge of financial matters.

You will also learn the chain of command that flows down through the rank officers, who are appointed by the post adviser. They are: chief, deputy chief, lieutenant, sergeant and quartermaster. Probably they are older members who have had two or three years' experience. They make sure you are ready for duty assignments, have the right equipment and are in uniform.

How do you get appointed chief or to any other position? You earn it several ways. These include:

- your record of attending weekly meetings,
- how you have handled duty assignments,
- training you have taken in various explorer jobs,
- how long you have been an explorer, and
- your scores on tests for promotion.

The officer who is post adviser and the civilian advisers weigh all that. They make the appointments.

UNIFORMS AND EQUIPMENT

You will have to buy a summer uniform and a winter uniform: long- and short-sleeved shirts with epaulets, trousers with piping, black shoes and socks, knit tie, web belt, police hat with visor and strap. You must also provide some basic equipment: flashlight, notepad, black-ink pens, whistle, name tag.

Maintaining all of this in good order—clean, polished, well pressed—is your responsibility.

ATTITUDE REQUIREMENTS

You have to have a real interest in law enforcement work and a dedication to it. The post is a democratic structure in the way post members elect peers as president, vice president and such. But it is a military or policelike structure in its chain of command from chief down through deputies and sergeants. So your attitude has to be, "OK, I can deal with this peer discipline."

SCHOLASTIC REQUIREMENTS

No police chief wants to get a call from a school principal saying, "Hey, you've got so-and-so in your Explorer Post, and it's a real distraction. This kid is flunking one course after another."

Most Explorer Posts state in their bylaws that a member must maintain a C average or better in school. But if you're having trouble, and your post adviser knows you're trying hard, he or she will try to get tutoring help for you.

CHAPTER FOUR
Summer Police Academy

*B*esides the weekly training, you can opt for intensive training at a Law Enforcement Explorer Academy. A typical academy is held for a week each summer at the Westover Air Force Base in Massachusetts. The session draws teenagers from all over New England and as far as Maryland and Ohio.

TRAINING LEVELS
The academy offers four levels of training:
- Phase One—first year,
- Phase Two—second year,
- Phase Three—third year, and
- Phase Four—last year.

Phase One. During your first year, you spend about 80 hours learning the basics of police work. You study juvenile justice, constitutional law, how to make an arrest and how to investigate a crime scene. You take plenty of notes, for you will face tough exams at the end of the week.

Outside the classroom, on the firing range, you learn gun safety. You drill and march to and from classes. Each evening, you sit down for a study period before lights-out at 10:30.

Phase Two. The program is more intense in your second year. You practice the real hands-on stuff. You investigate motor vehicle accidents. You find out how fatal accidents are handled. You explore crime scenes. You search buildings and in the field for evidence and for witnesses.

You also go to the firing range several times. With the teaching officers watching carefully, you shoot at targets in competition.

Phase Three. In your third year, you become a member of the academy's police department. You work on patrol, in uniform, as if you were in a regular police department.

You take your turns at the "midnights"—the late shifts, midnight until dawn. Now the teaching officers throw scenarios at you. One minute it's, "I locked my keys in my car," next it's a domestic dispute, then a burglary in progress. After that, someone is having a stroke or a fistfight breaks out over a fender bender. Each time, you are being trained to follow basic procedures and use restraint. You keep your cool.

During free time between shifts, you may go to the firing range. If there is room on the firing line, you can get familiar with various weapons, including the machine gun. But you are always paired off, one on one, with a police officer who is a certified range instructor.

Phase Three is so intense you may repeat it the next summer. You were a patrol officer last year, remember. Now you get tested for promotion, possibly to captain, or detective or chief of the department—the top honor of the week.

I've had people in the Explorer Academy program get hired right out from under me.
—Officer Matthew McNally

Phase Four. This reveals whether you are serious about going into law enforcement. Most of the explorers who attend Phase Four have completed high school and are at least 18. You go through tough workouts—running hard, tackling obstacle courses, proving you have the strength and stamina to be a police officer.

You take polygraph (lie detector) tests. You puzzle over one written test after another. You are dead serious, because you know federal agents are visiting, scouting for candidates to fill future jobs. And the police who are teaching are looking for future officers to tell their chiefs about.

Many posts hold fund-raisers to help send explorers to the academy.

COST OF THE ACADEMY

What does this cost? Who pays for it? A week for one explorer costs about $250 to $275. If you have saved some money, or if your parents can help—or both—you pay your own way. But many explorers welcome financial help. In fact, many posts hold fund-raisers to help send explorers to the academy.

CHAPTER FIVE

What's in It for You?

*W*hat can you gain by being a Police Explorer? The rewards and satisfactions range widely, including such learning experiences as:

- *Parliamentary procedure.* Weekly meetings teach you what *Robert's Rules of Order* says about who speaks when during a meeting.
- *Self-reliance.* You learn to recognize when you can, or must, take charge.
- *Teamwork.* You sharpen your skills in coordinating your efforts with others.

AN EXPLORER SHOWS SELF-RELIANCE

The scene: Running clubs are competing on a Sunday. Barricades edge the roadside, protecting runners who are using the highway's shoulder. Police Explorers direct traffic, freeing officers for other work.

Suddenly a car swerves through the barricade. It knocks down a runner. A teenage explorer is the first person at the car. She sees that the driver is drunk. She grabs the car keys so the driver can't drive away. She sees that the runner has a broken leg—a compound fracture. Certified in American Red Cross first aid, she goes to work.

"When we arrived," says a police officer, "that explorer was not only rendering first aid. She had the names of witnesses—everything—in her notebook. We told the chief what a fantastic job she did. The chief wrote her a letter of commendation."

(Bernard Ryan, Jr.)

David E. Haversat, three-year veteran volunteer at Police Explorer Post 130, Southbury, Connecticut, joins a patrol officer on a ride-along.

PRACTICAL EXPERIENCE

American Red Cross certification and cardiopulmonary resuscitation (CPR) are just two of the practical things you learn during your training sessions. Other experiences include:

- *Ride-alongs.* When you have completed 100 hours of service and reached the age of 16, you may ride in patrol cars with officers. You will learn what to do when a crime is "in progress." You will know when to assist the officer you ride with, and what to do if, in an emergency, you must be dropped off from the patrol car.

Ride-alongs are fun. I dreaded them at first. Eight hours in a car with a cop? What are we going to talk about? But I've seen some great things on a ride-along. The whole eight hours. You do everything.
                    —Police Explorer Bill Silva

- *Military.* Explorer work is sound premilitary experience. Recruits who have explorer backgrounds have been known to get their first stripes immediately upon induction into military service. Some post advisers go to recruitment headquarters with explorers who are enlisting. They want to make sure the enlistment officer understands the explorer's achievements and gives the explorer the best deal.
- *Forensic science.* "I've got kids here," says one adviser, "who know more about crime-scene investigation than most of the guys I work with." You learn many aspects of forensics, from how to find and retrieve fingerprints to analyzing blood spatters (their velocities and angles of trajectory).
- *Law.* Classroom sessions explain constitutional and criminal law. You find out how a police officer—especially since the famed Rodney King beating in Los Angeles—is supposed to make a decision on using force.
- *Other cultures.* You get many chances to learn about people who are different from you.
- *Fund-raising.* An Explorer Post must raise money to buy equipment.

Through fund-raising activities, you learn the techniques of asking for contributions—in person, by phone and through the mail.

AFTER–RODNEY KING POLICING

"You've got to use finesse, I tell the members of our post," reports Officer Matthew McNally, an adviser to a Police Explorer Post. "I talk to them about ARK (after–Rodney King) policing. I say, 'Listen, everybody's got a video camera. Think of it that way.' We videotape the training scenarios so that the explorers can see themselves. As we watch the videotapes we discuss what's happening. I'll say to them, 'See how you did this. What do you think about what you're doing?' And they say, 'Gee, I really made a mistake. I'm acting like a jerk here.' "

COLLEGE AND CAREER

On your applications for college, you will have the opportunity to describe specific experiences in handling explorer assignments that show your leadership and self-reliance. Include your certifications for CPR and first aid, too.

When it's time to look for jobs, you'll be glad you can put explorer experience on your applications. In fact, a number of explorers have moved directly into full- and part-time jobs in security. And if you want to go into professional police or fire-fighting work, the experience is invaluable.

Or suppose you decide to become a lawyer. What could look better on your application to law school than three or four years' experience as a Police Explorer?

FULFILLMENT

What else is in it for you? A number of things, including:

- A sense of accomplishment as you work closely with—and gain the respect of—professional men and women in law enforcement.
- Broadening your base of friendships into neighborhoods and cultures you haven't had a chance to know before.
- Helping younger teenagers learn the Explorer Post system.

(Bernard Ryan, Jr.)

High school senior Linda K. Carvalho has been a member of Law Enforcement Exploring Post 33, Danbury, Connecticut, since her sophomore year.

PEER PERCEPTIONS

"When my friends first saw me in my uniform, they said, 'Oh my God, look at you, you little blueberry!' " remarks Police Explorer Linda Carvalho.

"I came in here like any 15-year-old, and I expected to be laughed at. I was called Rent-a-cop and other names. But now, my friends are all OK with it. They admire my blue uniform.

"I've also met so many different people and learned so many different things," continues Carvalho. "I mean, my family—we're the Brady Bunch, right? And I come in here and I see these kids, these broken families, some parents who don't know how to speak English, and it's totally, totally different from what I'm used to. That opened up my mind."

- Moving upward through the chain of command to responsible leadership positions.

Perhaps most important of all, what's in it for you is the chance to find out whether law enforcement is a field you would like to work in for the rest of your life—as a police officer, an attorney or in a related job.

HOW DO YOU KNOW?

Is this area of community service the right one for you to volunteer in? And how do you join up? To get answers to such questions, be sure to read Part Four.

PART TWO
Volunteer Fire Fighting

CHAPTER SIX

The Junior Fire Corps

In a professional department, all firefighters must be at least 18 years old.

*W*hether you can be a teenage volunteer in a fire department may depend on whether your community maintains a paid staff of firefighters. If it does, you are not likely to find a Junior Fire Corps. Why not? Because in a professional department, all firefighters must be at least 18 years old.

But if you live where a volunteer fire company protects the community, it may boast a Junior Fire Corps or Explorer Post. Its members may be as young as 14. Once they turn 18, they may join the regular volunteer department.

The Junior Fire Corps is a self-governing organization. It has its own captain, first lieutenant, second lieutenant, supply sergeant, secretary and treasurer elected by the membership. Usually those officers are 17 or 18 and have been in the corps for three or four years.

The only qualification you need to be a Junior Fire Corps member is an interest in learning fire-fighting skills.

JUNIOR FIRE CORPS ADVISER

One or more adults serve as advisers. Often, an adviser is a firefighter who started in the corps during high school years. The adviser interviews applicants, plans the training activities (see chapter 7) and makes sure the corps officers are aware of events planned for the full department, so they can notify the junior membership.

(Vicki Harlow)

A Junior Fire Corps adviser is usually a firefighter who started volunteering as a teenager and continued as an adult. Jeremy Burr (standing), of Haddam, Connecticut's Volunteer Fire Department, conducts a training session with two juniors, showing them how to stabilize an automobile if an injured person has to be extricated from the vehicle.

CHAPTER SEVEN

What You'll Do in a Junior Fire Corps

*A*s a member of the Junior Fire Corps, you will have the opportunity to partici-pate in numerous fire-fighting activities, including training for fire and rescue sit-uations, being on the scene at actual fires and putting out brushfires. In addition, you can assist in fund-raising and participate in community and social events.

TRAINING

The adult members of the volunteer fire department include you in their training sessions. You also have training of your own, with your peers. Typical training includes:

- *Drills.* These are simulated fire and rescue situations. An old building that is to be torn down, for example, may be set up as a mock fire, filled with nontoxic smoke. Wearing an air tank, you practice entering the building and crawling through a maze. The drill simulates going through a fire in a house you've never been in before. You learn the best way to cut openings in the roof or knock out windows, to let out heat and smoke. Another type of drill involves setting up a pump truck at a lake or pond. Because this is not dangerous work, it is often given to Junior Fire Corps members in order to free up senior fire-fighters for more risky jobs.

(Vicki Harlow)

Training sessions include learning how to use all equipment needed during a real fire and rescue situation. Junior volunteer Mike Richmond mans the radio during a mock drill at Station #1, Haddam, Connecticut, Volunteer Fire Department.

If you're looking for water to put out a fire, you've got to find it right away—that's a critical job. We teach the older juniors how to operate the pump in case the engineer has a problem. They know how to call on the radio and how to shut the pump down.

—Volunteer Fire Chief Vincent A. Soares

- *Workshops.* The department will probably hold several workshops a year. You may learn radio communications so you know how fire, police and EMS units talk to each other. You learn CPR, how to handle such hazardous materials as chlorine and the best ways to deal with blood-borne pathogens (bacteria or viruses that can cause disease).
- *Maintenance.* Fire trucks, rescue vehicles and all their equipment must be kept ready for immediate use. That means regular cleaning, oiling, greasing, testing and replacing worn parts—whatever it takes. The firehouse must be spick-and-span, with a place for everything and everything in its place.

How do you learn these things? By showing up, one evening a week, when the senior volunteers go to the firehouse for vehicle maintenance and cleanup. There you clean the fire trucks and other apparatus. You sweep the firehouse floor. You

---

A LESSON IN GIVING

"The Junior Fire Corps offers no material reward, no pay," remarks Volunteer Fire Chief Vincent A. Soares. "It comes down to giving from the heart. We do it because we like to do it. Because we sincerely enjoy extending a helping hand. That goes from the most senior member down to the Junior Corps.

"We really start to train members to be firefighters in all the things that they can legally do—like ventilation, how to set fans up, what extension cords you need, where the equipment is on the truck."

(Bernard Ryan, Jr.)

Junior Fire Corps members (l-r): Second Lieutenant Dan Tomascak, Captain Ret Tolles and Joe Modeen at work moving and storing dried hoses during a Monday-evening maintenance meeting at the Southbury, Connecticut, Volunteer Fire Department.

help wash the tarpaulins that cover staging areas and protect property at a fire scene. You wash a hose, then roll it and pack it in the truck—just so, ready to unroll quickly.

This means getting your hands dirty, starting at the bottom and putting up with smelly stuff—like the odor of leftover smoke (in the hoses and tarpaulins and other gear) and cleaning solutions (detergents and solvents). But don't worry. You will not be asked to handle materials that are harmful.

WHEN THE ALARM SOUNDS

A volunteer fire department cannot let its junior members go into burning buildings, climb on roofs or operate power tools. But you will probably be allowed to ride in the truck, if there is room for you in the enclosed cab. Or you and other juniors may pile into the back of the rescue truck—a big box truck that is like a troop transport.

If you hear the alarm but get to the firehouse too late to ride in a truck, usually one of the members of the Ladies' Auxiliary will tell you to hop into her car. The firefighters want you there, because they count on you for help.

What do you do at the fire scene? You help set up the staging area—a central place for everybody to work from. You spread a tarpaulin on the ground. You carry tools from the trucks to this area. You lay out fresh air bottles, ready for when firefighters empty their breathing apparatus. You help unroll and hook up hose lines. You string out extension cords for power tools. If fire trucks and other apparatus are stretched out in a line—along a narrow road, for instance—some of the gear may be a quarter of a mile from the fire scene. You become a valuable runner, racing to get tools and equipment as the firefighters call for them.

THE LEARNING PROCESS

"When the juniors set up an airpack station at a structure fire, they get a chance to watch the evolution of a fire scene," says Volunteer Fire Chief Vincent A. Soares. "Even though fires are all different, each one contains the same elements—maybe not in the same order and not exactly the same faces and apparatus. But you learn a lot by watching."

When a firefighter wearing an airpack comes from the fire, you shut off the used air bottle, undo a hose, open a clamp, slide the used bottle out, slide a new bottle into the airpack and hook up the hose again. And off goes the firefighter back to the building.

(Vicki Harlow)

During a training session, familiarizing yourself with each piece of equipment will help you on the scene of a real fire. Juniors Mike Richmond and Franklin Pierce, from the Haddam, Connecticut, Volunteer Fire Department, check that all hoses are functioning properly.

The senior firefighters will encourage you to do something else at the fire scene: to watch. They want you to see how the fire scene is organized and the first hose line is stretched—how one crew goes inside the building, another crew goes to the roof to start a venthole and a backup crew stretches a second hose line.

In training sessions, you play the "go-find-a" game. You get abrupt orders to go find a tool or implement, or a switch or gauge on a truck, and stand by it until the senior firefighter who is running the drill comes to check you out. All of this helps you learn every detail of each fire truck, utility van, command vehicle, brush-fire truck or "hazmat" (hazardous materials) trailer. That means that when you are at a real fire scene and you are scurrying to get something from a truck, you know exactly what it is and where it is. You don't waste any time.

"Our juniors start at 16," says Sherman "Skip" Hardesty, chief of the Coles District Volunteer Fire Department in Manassas, Virginia. "They go through state-certified firefighting classes, and do everything except for actual interior firefighting, until they're 18. They're assigned to a rotating duty crew. That means one night a week and then one weekend a month. The juniors usually come on duty at 5:00 P.M. in the evening and stay until 10:00 P.M. weekdays, when school is on, during the week. In the summertime, as long as they have their parents' permission, they can bunk over—and the same on the weekends."

PUT THE WET STUFF ON THE RED STUFF

As a Junior Fire Corps volunteer, can you take the responsibility for actually putting out a fire?

Yes. Many volunteer companies encourage junior members to take charge of outdoor brushfires. In more than one case, in fact, it has been the juniors who recognized brushfires and called 911.

When you go to a brushfire, senior volunteers let you strap a five-gallon tank of water on your back. As you squirt water, you learn how to get the fire under control. You find out how to judge the way the wind is blowing and how fast the fire is spreading and where to head it off.

Brushfires are our fires. The brush truck is our truck, our baby.
We can get right in there and put the wet stuff on the red
stuff. That's fire slang—but it's kind of outdated.
         —Junior Fire Corps Adviser Heidi Roswell

FUND-RAISING

As a member of the Junior Fire Corps, you will want—and need—firefighters' boots, helmet and waterproof coat. The corps buys its own gear. It is not supported by the budget of the adult volunteer fire department. So your corps is likely to sponsor car washes and spaghetti dinners and candy-bar sales two or three times a year. These are usually good, fun activities and become annual events.

The corps may also send out a townwide mailing every year asking for support. Getting it written and printed, stuffing the envelopes and dealing with the post office will give you some valuable experience in raising money.

FUN AS WELL AS HARD WORK

The adult volunteers include the juniors not only in the hard work but also in the fun. You and your family can expect to be invited to the fire department's many social events—barbecues and cookouts, Super Bowl Sundays, Fourth of July and Labor Day celebrations and the annual open house at headquarters during Fire Prevention Week.

In the Memorial Day parade, your corps will probably march and may also mount a float—for instance, a replica of a burning house with nontoxic smoke coming from the department's practice machine inside. By dramatizing the corps' work, you help your fund-raising effort. What helps even more is when your corps marches in statewide parade competitions and wins first prizes.

CHAPTER EIGHT

What Does It Take to Work in a Junior Fire Corps?

*P*articipating in a Junior Fire Corps demands many of the same qualities you read about in chapter 3, on working in a Police Explorer Post. As a corps member, you must meet certain basic physical and mental requirements, attend weekly meetings, possess self-discipline, be responsible for your gear and maintain good grades in school.

You have to be willing to take orders.

PHYSICAL AND MENTAL REQUIREMENTS

Male or female, you must be in basic good health. Working the staging area at a fire calls for running back and forth and some heavy lifting.

Alcohol, tobacco and drugs cannot be part of your lifestyle.

You have to be willing to take orders. Organization is important. It makes the system work. So you must respect your peers who are captain, first lieutenant, second lieutenant and so on. And you must understand the adult chain of command at a fire scene. When seconds count in saving lives and property, you can't stand around wondering who's in charge or whom to obey.

BE THERE ONCE A WEEK

Regular attendance at meetings is a must. The juniors training session will probably start at 7:00 P.M. It should end by 9:00 P.M. if there is school the next day. At least once a month, training may be held for adult volunteers—either new members or experienced firefighters who are taking refresher training or learning about new techniques and equipment. You and the other Junior Fire Corps members can expect to be included.

(Vicki Harlow)

Haddam, Connecticut, Junior Fire Corps members meet once a week on Tuesday evenings. Juniors adviser Jeremey Burr (r) speaks to two volunteers, as Mike Vallera (standing), a former junior firefighter, adds his comments.

Duty assignments, of course, cannot be predicted. They come when the alarm goes off. You are expected to get there if you can. But don't expect to be excused from a classroom to rush to a fire.

ATTITUDE REQUIREMENTS

Your first assignment in the Junior Corps may be to sweep out the bays in the firehouse. Next you may be polishing up the shine on a truck. After that, you're washing down a messy tarpaulin spread out in front of the building.

How you handle the ordinary, basic, uninspiring tasks—better known as scut work—reveals how you handle self-discipline. It shows your willingness to take

(Vicki Harlow)

Mike Richmond, member of the Haddam, Connecticut, Junior
Volunteer Fire Corps, polishes the tanker at one of his weekly meetings.

orders both from adults and from your peers who have been elected officers of the corps. And it shows whether your work is neat and orderly, which the fire department wants, or tends to be sloppy, which it does not want.

BOOTS AND GEAR

What about uniforms? You will be issued boots, helmet and coat. It will be up to you to take them to meetings and to fire scenes. You must keep them clean and ready. Maintaining your gear is another test of your sense of responsibility, because the equipment belongs to the corps and was bought with money it raised.

SCHOOLWORK

You must maintain a C average or better in your schoolwork. That means finding time for homework, regardless of other demands. If you need help, your junior corps advisers will try to get tutoring for you. They don't want to lose you, and they don't want to lose the approval of the school authorities.

BASIC TRAINING

How much training you need and how old you have to be varies depending on where you are. Buzz Phelps, manager of the Society of National Fire Academy Instructors, knows volunteer fire departments across the country. He says, "There are different formats. One is the junior corps, where they limit the danger. In another, such as Maryland, when you're 16 you can be fully active and fight fires and go inside and all that good stuff—once you have a certain amount of training. Then there's other volunteer fire departments that don't take anybody unless they are 18 or even 21. Probably half say its OK to ride at 16 and do the full job to your level of training."

CHAPTER NINE
What's in It for You?

*K*nowing you are helping protect your community from fire is a reward in and of itself. But in learning how to do that, and in actually doing it, you gain many other rewards. Let's look at some.

DISCIPLINE AND SELF-RELIANCE

Much of what you will learn is like the Police Explorer experience. Participating in the weekly meetings teaches you parliamentary procedure and *Robert's Rules of Order.* Learning the system at a fire scene shows you the value of teamwork. Discovering the importance of good cleanup, orderliness and readiness takes you to new levels of self-discipline.

PRACTICAL

When you learn the fire-fighting system, you learn several separate systems that make it work. You find out about the chemistry of fire extinguishers. You discover how pumps work and how much power it takes to force water through a hose at high pressure to reach into a burning building. You become familiar with pressure gauges and the electrical power generated by a truck to operate power tools. You know how many gallons of water each truck holds and how long it will last at which pumping pressure.

You get to know local geography—what roads go where, which is the shortest route. You know not only where the lakes, ponds and streams are but also which are the most accessible to a giant tank truck.

Another key area you gain experience in is first aid and CPR. Most volunteer fire departments regularly schedule the American Red Cross first-aid course and CPR class for their members. Depending on your state's law, you may be certified at age 16.

(Bernard Ryan, Jr.)

During a Monday-evening maintenance meeting, Joshua R. Brown, treasurer of the Southbury, Connecticut, Volunteer Fire Department's Junior Fire Corps, checks out truck equipment.

As in the Police Explorers, you learn fund-raising, for you and your peers must raise the money to buy uniforms and equipment. When is the best time of year to raise money? Does telephoning work better than the mail? How much profit can you expect if 200 people show up for your spaghetti dinner? You gain experience you can use for years to come.

COLLEGE AND CAREER

Put your Junior Fire Corps experience on college and job applications. It can help you look good to an admissions officer and maybe win scholarship aid. Cite specifics: duties in which you were responsible for quick air-tank replacement, stringing hose or power lines, monitoring pressure gauges, cleaning up. Don't forget first-aid or CPR certification. And if you've been elected to leadership positions, make that clear, too.

On any job application, include details of your Junior Fire Corps experience. You want to show learning ability, leadership, dedication, dependability—all those good things employers look for.

THE FUN STUFF

"The Junior Fire Corps is not all sweeping, hose rolling and washing down tarpaulins," reports Heidi Roswell, a Junior Fire Corps adviser. "The juniors do do fun things," she points out.

"In the summer, we have musters that are like a fire-service competition, with all kinds of contests—bucket brigades, water polo, tugs-of-war to see who gets pulled into the stream from a fire hose. Ladder races, running portable pumps, midnight alarms—they get to do it all.

"And they're always invited, along with their parents and their whole families, to social events, like the Christmas party, the summer clambake, Super Bowl Sunday, and parades.

"They have their own uniforms, just like the regular firefighters. They're judged just the way we regular firefighters are."

SATISFACTIONS

Probably the most satisfying thing about being a Junior Fire Corps member is the sense of accomplishment you come home with when you have helped your volunteer fire department control and extinguish a serious fire, saving valuable property and perhaps even lives.

Other satisfactions you may experience include:

- You work closely with adult volunteers, earning their respect.
- You make new friends your own age.
- As you move upward through the system, you lead the younger members, helping them learn the ropes.
- By volunteering in this real-world activity, you find out whether you are interested in becoming a paid professional or a volunteer firefighter in your adult years.

PUNISHMENT LEADS TO THE FIREHOUSE

"I never really thought about being in the fire department," recalls Junior Fire Corps Captain Ret Tolles. "But when I was starting high school, I fell in with the wrong crowd. One guy convinced me to do things I wouldn't normally do and one day we had a little campfire and it spread.

"My punishment was to come down to the firehouse for a month to work it off. It was punishment at that time. But now I've been here the longest—almost three years—and it's preparing me for what I want to do when I get older.

"I especially like the way we all work together to make one perfect scene. One person may know the easiest way to set up a scut station, another may work faster at changing the airpacks. Whoever's best at one thing, that's what works, and we get it done. And we help the new people who don't know as much as we do."

IS IT RIGHT FOR YOU?

To weigh whether this kind of community service matches your own interests and capabilities, and to find out how to volunteer for it, see Part Four.

GETTING IN ON THE ACTION

"The teenagers usually come in when they are 14," says Fred Allinson, Battalion Chief of a volunteer fire company in a King County suburb outside Seattle, Washington. "They start in an Explorer Post and have their own association and do their own thing. They train on drill night, one night a week. If we get a call and it's a real working fire and the guys are going to be there for a long time, we'll call the dispatcher and ask them to send an Explorer Post. They have a van they bring out, and they make hot chocolate and coffee and have some candy bars and goodies for the fire fighters. We used them just two weeks ago, in the middle of the night.

"They're a great help. For example, a guy comes out—they can only stay in through one air bottle—and he goes through re-hab and everything, and he usually wants something to drink, and these teens have it there for him. And they can replace air bottles, depending on the department they're affiliated with. You might have one department that lets the teens do certain things, and the next department down the road might not let them. So it depends."

EMS TRAINING, TOO

In many volunteer fire departments, fire fighters are trained as emergency medical technicians (EMTs) and the community's Emergency Medical Service (EMS) is provided—and dispatched—through the fire service. Often, teens in the Junior Corps or Explorer Post can take classes alongside the adult firefighters and become certified in first aid and as EMTs, depending on the age limitations set by the states in which they live. See Part Three for more on teens in the EMS.

Voluntary Emergency Service Work

CHAPTER TEN

Emergency Medical Service Explorers

*H*ere's that word "explorer" again. Why? Because the teenage volunteer chapters of some Emergency Medical Service (EMS) units, like some Police Explorer divisions, grew out of the Boy Scouts of America's Explorer Division. So teens in the EMS often belong officially to their community's EMS Explorer Post. To be an EMS explorer, however, you do not have to be a Boy Scout or a Girl Scout.

IMPORTANCE OF TEEN EMS VOLUNTEERS

The opportunity to serve in the EMS is either very limited or very open, depending on where you live.

You should understand two basic facts about EMS Explorer Posts. First, this is a growing field for teen volunteers. Many smaller communities depend on volunteers to run not only their fire departments but their emergency medical services. But, with both partners working full-time, many households nowadays find they cannot make very much adult volunteer time available. In more and more communities, young adults—that is, teens—provide an untapped resource.

Second, the opportunity to serve in the EMS is either very limited or very open, depending on where you live. Why? Because laws about medical matters vary state to state and even locally. For example, in Connecticut and several other states, you are eligible at 16 to be certified in CPR and as a Medical Response Technician (MRT) or, more advanced, an Emergency Medical Technician (EMT). In some states, you have to be 18 or even 21.

THE ADVANTAGES OF HAVING TEEN VOLUNTEERS

Bill Ackley, an adult adviser to an Explorer Post in Stratford, Connecticut, recalls how the use of teen volunteers in the town's EMS program began. "Back in 1991, my wife and I took a look at how we could broaden the resources of the volunteer system. One of the areas we looked at was the Explorer Post. It's gained us between 20 and 30 additional members.

"One of the advantages of teenagers is that they're available when other people may not be. The service reaps the benefits of school vacations, summer vacations. They come in at two o'clock right after school. Before, with people working, we couldn't cover our busiest time—between one-thirty and five in the afternoon. The teens cover that time, so the service benefits tremendously."

EMS EXPLORER POST MAKEUP

In a typical EMS Explorer Post, you will find a maximum of about 50 teens. The youngest is at least 14 and in at least ninth grade in high school. From 10 to 20 adults serve as advisers or as members who participate equally with the teens in operating the post. Teens and adults have equal voting rights, but only teens are elected as officers: president, vice president of programming, vice president of training, vice president of operations, secretary and treasurer.

EMS—EXCITEMENT AND ENTHUSIASM

"Teen volunteers give the EMS a younger, energetic group of people who are there because they want to be there," says EMS Explorer Rick Weismiller. "Everything is exciting for us, every call, every little thing. Just the fact that we get to drive an ambulance is exciting. Turning on ambulance lights, turning on switches in the back, helping someone.

"Having that enthusiasm in younger kids—it's great for the EMS system. Even the chief of police went on television and said he believes that a lot of us are even more skilled when we answer emergency calls than the police officers who also answer."

CHAPTER ELEVEN

What You'll Do as an EMS Explorer

*L*et's look at one of the most successful EMS operations in America—Post 53, in Darien, Connecticut. Founded in 1970, it operates three ambulances and a Jeep called the "fly car" (because it "flies" to an emergency even faster than the ambulance). All are housed in a white headquarters building constructed with money the post raised. From this location, its teen volunteers respond to about a thousand 911 calls a year.

Post 53 has won many honors, including a National Award for Excellence from the American Medical Association. It has been designated "one of the top ten volunteer organizations in the U.S." and was named one of President George Bush's 1,000 "daily points of light" in 1992.

MEDICAL RESPONSE TECHNICIAN AND EMERGENCY MEDICAL TECHNICIAN

At Post 53, you start as a *candidate* for three months. Your sponsor—an older teen—helps you get ready. Within those 90 days, instructors train you as an MRT. The 40-hour course teaches you the procedures in Basic Life Support (BLS) that you need at any medical emergency. You learn CPR (restoring heartbeat and breathing), airway clearance (breathing), hemorrhage control (bleeding), protection of skeletal injuries (broken bones) and emergency childbirth.

After you pass a test by the state's Office of Emergency Medical Services, you are a certified MRT. And your sponsor presents you to the membership, which votes you in. They judge you on attitude, ability with first aid, character, personal

(Bernard Ryan, Jr.)

In Darien, Connecticut, Post 53, the EMS "fly car" is its fastest vehicle, arriving on the accident scene ahead of the ambulance.

commitment, dependability and overall helpfulness. (See Appendix A for Post 53's sample congratulatory letter to a candidate as well as its candidate checklist and guidelines for sponsors.)

You barely catch your breath, for you immediately start a 110-hour course to become an EMT, a higher level of training that goes beyond BLS. It enables you to provide more complex treatment.

Becoming an MRT and then an EMT may take well over a year, at a rate of one training session a week.

WHO DOES WHAT

In the training program, you begin learning several jobs, including:

- *Radio roomie.* In this key spot, you control all communication in the post's radio room. You answer telephones and radio calls and keep records of them. You make sure all portable radios and pagers are operating properly.

- *Ambulance rider.* Here, you anticipate what equipment will be needed during a call and assist wherever you are asked or obviously needed. You replenish supplies. You empty garbage.

- *Ambulance driver.* Now you make sure the ambulance is ready—lights, sirens, radios, gas, tires, body. If it is dirty, you clean it. When a call comes, you drive the ambulance to the scene and to the hospital—speedily but safely, not recklessly. At the scene, you help with patient care.

- *EMT.* With this title, you direct the care of the patient or patients, and take responsibility for radio communications. This includes making sure all radios—portables and those in the ambulances—are turned on with the volume up.

- *Crew chief.* In this spot, you check out all supplies and medical equipment. Before every call, you grab fresh ice packs from the post refrigerator and put them in the cooler in the ambulance. At the emergency scene, you handle overall supervision and control.

Usually each ambulance carries a crew of four. Two more go in the fly car. Once you are a certified EMT, you may be assigned any one of the four ambulance jobs. They usually rotate. For example, if you are EMT on one tour of duty, you may be driver on another, rider on the next, and crew chief on the one after that. While all on the crew may be certified EMTs, one is designated "the EMT" on each duty assignment.

How often do you do a 24-hour tour? The minimum at Post 53 is two each month. Many explorers do more than that.

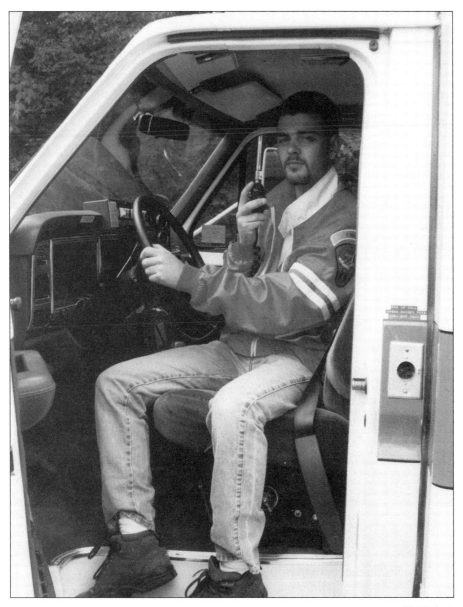

(Vicki Harlow)

At the Haddam, Connecticut, Volunteer Ambulance Association's headquarters, the base radio is located directly in the ambulance for the best reception. Volunteer Shawn Archer signs on for his evening shift.

LISTEN IN ON A CREW MEETING

Following is a verbatim transcript (the actual words said) as high school senior Tania Nisimblat led a crew meeting as a 24-hour tour of duty got under way. Tania, as driver, reviewed each person's assignments in various possible situations. The ambulance crew was three teens and one adult, with two teens in the fly car.

"Bobby is our EMT. Our rider is Faraday, Mrs. Brownlee is crew chief. In the event of an MVA [motor vehicle accident] on the interstate, I'll wait for the fire department or Mary [in the fly car] to let me know it's OK to get on the scene. When we get there, you guys stay inside until I say it's OK to get out.

"Faraday, you strip the stretcher and put the backboard on. Don't forget the extrication straps and blanket rolls. Bobby, you can get out [of the ambulance] with your patient care. Mrs. Brownlee will help you. Faraday and I will do equipment. If there's a two-patient split, it will be Bobby and Mary, Faraday and Mrs. Brownlee. Three-patient split will be Bobby and myself and Mrs. Brownlee. If there's an airless [not breathing] patient, you get that and then next severe and next severe and I'll call for 54 [the second-response ambulance].

"In the event of a cardiac, I'll just make sure there's a lot of communication. Look in the back of the fly car to make sure what she has and let's not forget suction and portables. Bobby, you can go in and take over airway. We'll have the cop doing CPR on the chest until we get to the ambulance and we can take over. I'll do equipment and running back and forth to get you guys stuff.

"In the event of a call to the nursing home, I'll stay downstairs with the ambulance. Make sure you guys pile everything on the stretcher and then take it up. If it's

(Continued on page 55)

(Continued from page 54)

in the middle of the night, we'll make sure Alex [coming on duty later] props the door open. Do as much as you can in the ambulance. We don't want to waste time upstairs there, it takes so much time in the elevators.

"House calls, try not to crowd the room. But maybe Faraday can do more stuff, since she's almost an EMT. I'll do more equipment stuff, so don't worry about that. And Bobby and Beth [from the fly car], maybe you can help out with patient care. Whatever you can do in the ambulance, do in the ambulance rather than in the home. Do a blood pressure in the ambulance if it's BLS. Don't waste time in the home. Let's just get going. Just do things, don't wait to be told. Work fast."

CHAPTER TWELVE

What Does It Take to Be an EMS Explorer?

As an EMS Explorer, you must meet certain basic physical and attitude require-ments, attend training and membership meetings and maintain good grades in school.

PHYSICAL REQUIREMENTS

In most states, the health department requires that all ambulance personnel be physically fit, capable of helping lift a stretcher carrying a patient. Once a year you must have your family doctor certify that you are fit. (See Appendix B for a sam-ple medical form.)

In addition, you (or your parents, if you are under 18) must sign a form show-ing that you either have been immunized against Hepatitis B, in the post's health program, or have refused the series of shots. (See Appendix B.)

On a random basis every month, several people—candidates, members and adults—are picked without warning for urinalysis. If the tests reveal any illegal drug in your system, you are immediately relieved of duty and advised to get counseling.

The use of alcoholic beverages is also forbidden. Smoking tobacco is discouraged.

ATTITUDE REQUIREMENTS

In operating radio communications, riding ambulances and serving ill or injured patients, you are being given adult responsibilities. They call for a totally profes-

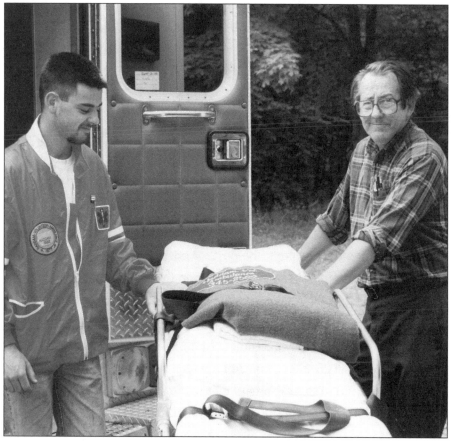

(Vicki Harlow)

At Haddam, Connecticut's Volunteer Ambulance Association, junior volunteers meet once a week for training. Here, adviser Tom Kobylenski instructs volunteer Shawn Archer on how to prepare a stretcher.

sional attitude. For example, any officer may appoint you to some specific job, and you may ask any other member of the post to help. Any member who refuses to help when asked is subject to review by the elected officers, and may be dismissed from membership.

Information about the care of any patient, and about all post business, is super confidential. You discuss such matters with *no one*—not your family, not your friends. Some things you learn about people you help, or events you witness, may be strictly police or hospital information. It can be released only by sub-poena—that is, a court order.

Ambulance emergencies bring stress, whether you expect it or not. The regular procedure after every call includes a critique, and the critique includes the management of stress. Talking out your innermost thoughts with others who have been in the same situation, and whose training is the same, is usually quite effective. If the stress is unusually severe, you can get more help through your post counselor and the hospital your post serves.

TRAINING AND ATTENDANCE REQUIREMENTS

Training usually means being at the post for one evening at least every other week. Often a membership meeting is held on the same evening in alternate weeks—so you are committed to one evening a week. But training never ends. You have to pass tests for reaccreditation regularly, and new medical developments and techniques are always coming along.

Probably you will do at least one 24-hour tour of duty every other week. You report at the post by 5:30 P.M., attend the crew meeting, check out equipment and respond to 911 calls through the evening. While standing by for calls, you stay at headquarters, doing homework, watching TV, hanging out. You go home at midnight, with your beeper, and respond from home if needed during the night. Next day, you go to school with your beeper. Each post member is allowed to respond to one call during school time, so the schedule tells others when they are on "second response" and "third response" after you. After school, you go straight to the post to be on duty until 5:30.

SCHOLASTIC REQUIREMENTS

The EMS Explorer Post expects you to maintain a C average, or better, in school. If your marks fall below that, your school will probably put you on academic probation and notify the post's president. You will then not be allowed to take any duty assignment during school hours or school-day evenings.

CHAPTER THIRTEEN
What's in It for You?

By now, you may be thinking, "Wow! This EMS stuff is a lot of responsibility! What's in it for *me*?"

The answer lies in four basic areas:

1. the discipline of teamwork,

2. practical experiences,

3. college and career, and

4. personal satisfaction.

THE DISCIPLINE OF TEAMWORK

In an EMS Explorer Post, a tremendous amount of discipline is imposed on you. Call it peer discipline or group discipline. It sets standards you must meet constantly and without exception. The reward? You find out how much you and others can accomplish through teamwork.

As you work to ease pain and save lives, you gain self-reliance. Winning CPR and EMT certification tells you that you can handle complex, stressful emergencies—medical or otherwise.

PRACTICAL EXPERIENCE

If you think you might want to be a doctor or a nurse or do other work in the medical field, you can't beat the EMS experience as a way to find out if it is right for you and you are right for it. And the certifications you gain—in first aid, CPR, MRT and EMT—give you a background in handling medical emergencies that you can use all your life, even if you do not keep your certification up to date or pursue a career in the medical field.

You get other practical experience you can use for years. Every EMS Explorer Post does its own fund-raising to buy needed equipment. If you're a member, you participate. You learn the techniques of direct-mail and telephone solicitation.

GAINING EXPERIENCE

"Not only do you get the experience of almost being in the medical field, but there's so much the post gives each of us," says Alexandra Bisset, president of EMS Explorer Post 53. "While we don't feel above the other kids in high school, we've experienced things they can never imagine. I mean, there are times when we've been up all night on the interstate, just doing our job. And we get to school the next day and some kid is complaining that he didn't get enough sleep because he had to write a paper. And you want to say, 'You have no idea what you're talking about.' "

COLLEGE AND CAREER

Your EMS experience has real value on your application for college or for a job. It can help you earn scholarship aid. It can open the door to part- or full-time jobs in EMS work, nursing and other areas of medicine.

SATISFACTIONS

Certainly helping to treat injuries and illness, relieve pain and save lives can give you great satisfaction. Beyond that, you gain the satisfaction of serving your community. You also gain knowledge and experience that you can pass on to younger teens who are learning the system. And, of course, few satisfactions can beat that of running a valuable adult program with your peers and with a minimum of adult supervision.

(Vicki Harlow)

Shawn Archer began volunteering with Haddam, Connecticut's Volunteer Ambulance Association at age 17.

PUTTING TRAINING TO THE TEST

"I got my EMT card when I was 16," says EMS Explorer Ben Corb. "When I apply for college I will have been an EMT for two years. I've been able to do this while in high school and that shows responsibility, credibility and character.

"There are times when I'd rather be working for money or just hanging out with my friends instead of giving up an entire weekend or a whole Saturday. But I tell myself I decided to give up the time to get the certification, so why not take advantage of it?"

Ben Corb called on his EMT certification and training in the summer after 10th grade, when he and other EMS explorers returning from an explorer picnic witnessed a severe accident.

"A car with five people in it flipped over," Corb says. "We were the first on the scene. We helped all the injured. The patient I mainly took care of was the driver. His injuries were pretty bad, and he ended up dying from them."

A few months later Corb and the other explorers were given a proclamation from the town council for dedication and professionalism. According to Corb, the EMS training pays off even when you don't anticipate needing it. He notes, "Even though the person I took care of didn't make it, it made me feel good that of all the cars that were on the highway, not many responded. But we did. And we worked and saved who we could."

CHAPTER FOURTEEN
Related Volunteer Services

*Y*ou can find other volunteer services that welcome teenagers and deal with crisis situations. Some communities have formed individual programs. For example, in Warm Springs, Oregon, the Search and Rescue Cadet program puts kids ages 10 to 18 to work helping the Jefferson County Search and Rescue team. The cadets learn first aid, CPR, water rescue and wilderness survival.

Contact your local police, fire department or state police to find out if such programs exist where you live. Remember, use the blue pages in your phone book to find the numbers for "routine calls." Do not call 911.

CIVIL AIR PATROL CADET PROGRAM

Across the United States, more than 18,000 boys and girls participate in the Civil Air Patrol (CAP) program. Cadet ages range from 12 to 21.

The program not only introduces you to the wonders of aviation,but it also takes you through a range of activities—survival training, search-and-rescue techniques, disaster relief, the "how-to's" of radio communication, first aid and CPR, astronomy, model rocketry and flight training in both powered and glider aircraft. About 10 percent of the students in the U.S. Air Force Academy are former CAP cadets.

CAP SERVICES

The CAP functions in every state, providing many services, including:
- *Search and rescue.* The CAP flies more than 85 percent of all inland (not over the ocean) missions directed by the U.S. Air Force Rescue Coordination

(Courtesy: Civil Air Patrol)

Civil Air Patrol (CAP) cadets participate in "Survival Training" in Montgomery, Alabama, in October 1996. The program was part of a two-week training session made available to 102 qualified cadets through scholarship funding.

Center. It saves more than 100 people every year.

- *Disaster relief.* When a flood, hurricane or tornado strikes, the CAP provides air and ground transportation and communications coordinated with other rescue and relief efforts.
- *Humanitarian services.* CAP planes fly blood, human tissue and organs for transplants where other transportation is too slow.
- *Countering drug operations.* Aerial reconnaissance, communications and air-lifting of law enforcement people are supplied by the CAP in the continuing war on drugs.

(Courtesy: Civil Air Patrol)

Civil Air Patrol cadets prepare to assist with crowd control at the Alabama Air Show held at Maxwell Air Force Base in Montgomery, Alabama, in December 1996.

To find the CAP headquarters nearest you and to inquire about the Cadet program, phone 1-800-FLY-2338, check out http://www.cap.af.mil on the Internet, or write to:

> National HQ, Civil Air Patrol
> Membership Development
> 105 South Hansell Street, Bldg. 714
> Maxwell AFB, AL 36112-6332

PART FOUR

Making Your Decision and Joining Up

CHAPTER FIFTEEN

Is It Right for You?

*B*y now, you are probably asking yourself, "Is one of these services right for me?" To get an answer, you must consider some of the advantages and satisfactions that come from dealing successfully with stress, emergencies and crises. And you must think about the disadvantages and dissatisfactions, too.

To help you make a decision, take the self-quiz at the end of this chapter and see where you come out.

ADVANTAGES AND SATISFACTIONS

Most teens who volunteer to help in crisis or near-crisis situations say they like the sense of accomplishment they gain. They reach an understanding of what happens to people in trouble—how human beings react when they must deal with an accident, injury, fire or crime or crisis situation. And they gain an understanding of how good it feels to help others.

Knowing you are helping people, seeing the relief on their faces when you and other teen volunteers help get a fire under control, relieve pain or just help get stalled traffic moving—nothing beats that.

Working with police, fire and EMS crews, you become aware that you are earning acceptance by your peers and by adults. Teachers, you find, are aware of what you are doing. They respect you for it. Overall, in any of these programs, you improve your self-image.

When you're an explorer, the teachers know about you. They expect you to be more responsible, more upstanding. They expect you to speak up, to be more assertive, because you have a lot of responsibilities when you're a Police Explorer.

—Police Explorer Kyron Ward

There's also the fun stuff. The parades. The summertime barbecues and picnics, the winter holidays and Super Bowl Sunday parties. Beyond the duty assignments, the social side is quite enjoyable. It's like belonging to a special club.

The relaxing social life helps relieve the constant pressure of being ready to deal with an emergency. Most volunteer fire departments, for example, maintain (and get a lot of use out of) broad patios with overhead canopies behind the firehouse, complete with fireplace grills and picnic tables. They know how to have a good time.

Does it cut into your social life? No, it's part of your social life. The part it cuts out, it sort of answers in some way. You're friends with the kids who are in here. You hang out with them.

— EMS Explorer Rick Weismiller

DISADVANTAGES AND DISSATISFACTIONS

Let's face it—there are some disadvantages to think about.

1. *No pay.* The hours you spend in any voluntary or mandatory community service don't earn you any money. They come out of your free time. So you have to think about how you spend all your time outside of school—on part-time jobs, homework, household chores, sleeping, eating and hanging out.

2. *Peer pressure.* You may have to face peers who poke fun at you, at least in the beginning. Most Police and EMS Explorers and Junior Fire Corps

members find that their peers soon accept what they are doing and— some sooner, some later—admire them for it.

3. *Weather.* Much of the work is done outdoors, in fair and foul weather, hot and cold. There's nothing colder than the freezing spray of a fire hose or the ice underfoot at a winter fire. Nor is there anything hotter than being inside boots, helmet and waterproof coat on a steamy summer day. And that's not to mention directing traffic or helping an accident victim onto a stretcher and into an ambulance in a teeming downpour. If you can't stand being out in uncomfortable weather, you don't want any of these jobs.

4. *Uniform cost.* You provide your own uniform and basic equipment, costing up to $200. Why must you provide them? Because, the advisers figure, you are more likely to take care of them if you paid for them. Some posts and corps, however, are supported by individuals or corporations that help pay for uniforms and equipment.

5. *Code of conduct.* Is it a disadvantage for you to meet a code of conduct that many of your peers may not be meeting? No tobacco and no alcohol if you are under the legal age for them. No drugs—period. And your peer group administers the discipline.

SELF-QUIZ

As you think about what or whether community service is right for you, check these questions:

• Do you have a broad interest in the field of law and law enforcement?

• How about an interest in helping people who are injured or in trouble, and in saving property as well as lives?

• Can you keep all prejudices out of your work—cooperate with people of all religious, racial and ethnic backgrounds?

• Are you a team player?

• Can you handle strict rules and a code of conduct?

• Can you keep confidential information to yourself?

- Can you work cooperatively with members of the opposite sex?
- Can you put up with peer pressure that teases, mocks, puts you down?
- Can you act with authority toward peers, yet be friends with them?
- Can you keep calm and cool amid chaos and confusion? Follow procedures you've been trained in, despite pressure and distraction?
- How squeamish are you? Do you have the stomach for dealing with people who are injured, bleeding, unclean or emotionally upset?
- Will you work hard to maintain good grades in school, so you can stay in the volunteer group?
- Can you devote at least one evening a week, and maybe several hours on weekends, to this activity?
- Can you be on call for emergencies at any time, day or night—except when you are in school? And even in school, if you join an EMS Explorer Post?
- Are you thinking of a career in medicine or related fields, or as an adult member of an EMS unit?

CHAPTER SIXTEEN

How to Join Up

WHERE TO CALL AND WHAT TO SAY

If you want to know whether your police department, volunteer fire department or EMS has an Explorer Post or Junior Fire Corps, give them a call. But don't dial 911. Look in your phone book's blue pages, under the listings of city or town offices, for the number for "routine calls" to the service you want.

If they say they have a post or junior corps, ask for the person who is the adviser. If you can't reach him or her right then, leave a message saying you want to find out about joining the post. Be sure to include your name and phone number. Ask if the adviser can mail you an application form. Or offer to stop by the headquarters and pick up the form.

The adviser is sure to be busy and overworked. So if no one calls within a few days, call again. Don't be afraid to keep calling. A good adviser will be glad you are persistent. They're not looking for wimps.

HOW TO APPLY

The typical application form is very simple. It will probably ask only for your name, address, age and grade in school.

Probably the organization's adviser and its president (a high school junior or senior, remember, elected by his or her peers) will ask you to come in for an interview. You can expect it to be friendly and brief.

Be ready for routine questions about your family, how long you've lived in the community, your grade level in school and what school subjects you like best.

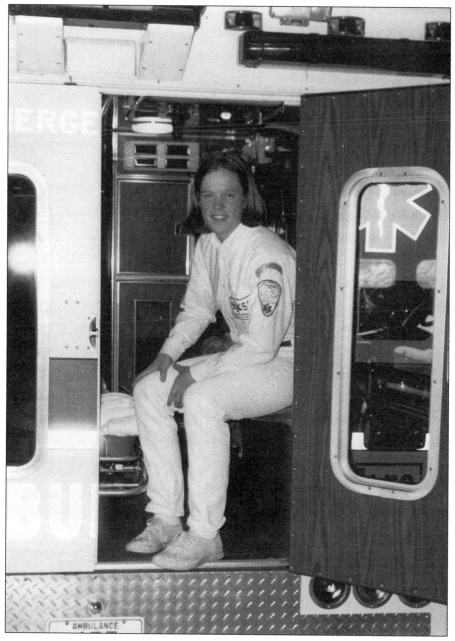

(Bernard Ryan, Jr.)

Alexandra Bisset, president, EMS Explorer Post 53, Darien, Connecticut, is a senior in high school.

They will want to know if you are thinking ahead toward this particular field as a career. That's not a must, by the way. To be eligible as a teen volunteer, you are not required to be headed for a career in that area. (If you are looking into EMS work, see Appendix A for a candidate checklist.)

And you can ask questions. Use this book to guide you on questions to ask. You'll want to find out when the meetings are held, and for how long. Ask how many members there are, both male and female. What ages are they? How many advisers? What are some of the duties and assignments? What will you be doing when you first join? Is there a period of probation, and how long is it? How much will your uniform cost? How about equipment—what must you provide? Let them know you have thought about it and have sound questions.

PREPARE YOUR RÉSUMÉ

Take along a résumé. Preparing one gives you two advantages. First, it makes you think about things to cover in the interview. Second, it tells the adviser you know how to think about where you have been and what you have done.

On your résumé, include your full name, address, age, grade in school and school activities (for example, Key Club, drama club, sports teams, science club, 4-H Club, publications, etc.). And don't forget part-time jobs, from baby-sitting to delivering newspapers to mowing lawns and shoveling snow. You want the reader of your résumé to see how well-rounded you are.

LOOK YOUR BEST

Your personal appearance is important in the interview. Leave the grunge look at home. Clean, freshly pressed clothing makes a good impression. Take a cue from one Explorer Post's bylaws on physical appearance and grooming. While these rules are from a Police Explorer Post, they could apply just as well to an EMS Post or Junior Fire Corps.

Think of your interview for membership in a post or junior corps as a job interview, for that is just what it is. Look your best. Speak your best.

All explorers will be physically clean when reporting for a detail or activity, especially when in full uniform. Hands and fingernails will be free of any paint, grease or other substances.

All explorers are expected to have their hair clean, combed and presentable at all times.

All explorers must remove all loose jewelry for safety.

All male explorers will have their hair neatly trimmed, cut to collar length or above and combed at all times.

All male explorers are expected to be clean shaven when in full uniform. Mustaches are allowed but must be kept neatly trimmed.

All female explorers are required to wear their hair up in a bun, ponytail or French braid while in full uniform.[2]

[2] Source: Southbury, Connecticut, Police Explorer Post 130 bylaws

When they start going for jobs, people say, Gee, you're a
Police Explorer? They know they're getting someone who has
some idea of what they're doing.
—Officer Matthew McNally, Police Explorers Adviser

DIVERSITY—A KEY TO SUCCESS

One 20-year-old Police Explorer Post was floundering, down to only six teenagers, when Matthew McNally took over as adviser in 1991. Within three years, membership grew to 36, and by 1997 it was nearly 60.

McNally's secret? He treats every teen the same. "We try to identify kids who are interested in the program," he says, "and we also try to identify kids who are kind of

(Continued on page 76)

(Continued from page 75)

lost in the crowd. They're looking for somebody to hang with. I sell the program as a family. My kids are diverse, from all walks of life, all religions, all ethnic backgrounds."

McNally also helps with jobs and colleges. Companies looking for security guards call him, asking, "You got any explorers who are 18 or older?" College deans and registrars also call him regarding candidates' applications. They say, "Listen, no way this kid could have done all this." McNally says, "I've got a file on every kid. You want me to send you the whole file? If it says my explorer did 1,400 hours of community service in the past three years, my explorer did 1,400 hours."

Post 53's Congratulatory Letter, Candidate Checklist and the Role of a Sponsor

CONGRATULATORY LETTER

Dear Candidate,

Congratulations! You have been selected as a candidate for membership in a nationally famous young adult organization, Explorer Post 53. At Post 53 we are professionals striving to provide the highest quality of emergency care to citizens of our community. We are a very close family working together year-round to support and maintain our organization.

Your candidacy is a period of three months during which we, the Post members, get to know you and you get to know us. To help guide you as a newcomer, you have been assigned a sponsor who is an officer and/or a senior member of the post. It is the responsibility of you both to develop an open relationship and to work together towards your acceptance for membership. Your sponsor will represent you when the officers and the other members discuss your recommendation for membership.

The following checklist is to give you an idea of what we expect of you as a candidate. It is not meant to intimidate you but to guide you in becoming a member of our family. Please read the list carefully and discuss any questions you have with your sponsor. Halfway through your candidacy your sponsor will use this list to evaluate you based on his/her own observations and feedback from the rest of the members. At the end of your candidacy you will go through this evaluation process again, and your sponsor will then use this as a basis for discussing your acceptance for membership.

Congratulations again and welcome to Post 53.

Sincerely,

The Members and Advisers of Post 53

CANDIDATE CHECKLIST

1. Candidate attends all scheduled post business meetings and training sessions during the three months of candidacy, unless Candidate has a major conflict and has been excused.
2. Candidate attends all scheduled work parties during the three months.
3. Candidate strives to develop an open relationship with sponsor and takes the initiative to ask the sponsor or post member questions concerning his/her candidacy.
4. Candidate displays an attitude of respect toward every officer, adult adviser and member of Post 53.
5. Candidate accepts responsibilities at work parties and on duty and proves dependable in completing each task.
6. Candidate assures his/her sponsor, the officers and the advisers of Post 53 that his/her parents fully understand the commitment and total personal responsibility involved in belonging to Post 53.
7. Candidate proves capable of handling his/her commitment to Post 53 along with other extracurricular activities such as athletics, theater, school newspaper, student government, etc.
8. Candidate is alert at all times when on duty and can answer questions concerning a call or what is happening on the radios accurately and concisely.
9. Candidate fully understands the bylaws and house rules of Post 53.
10. Candidate demonstrates pride in being a member of Post 53 by adhering appropriately to dress codes and to the bylaws during any post activity and at any time while representing us in the community.
11. Candidate realizes that any patient information, police information and Post 53 business is confidential and must not be discussed with any non-member.
12. Candidate learns the radio room equipment and procedures and thus passes the radio room test when he/she is ready within the candidacy period.

13. Candidate strives to develop a professional working relationship with the members of Post 53 during duty, training sessions and all post activities.

14. Candidate demonstrates a continuing acceptable level of skill and knowledge in basic first aid and CPR during training sessions.

15. Candidate performs appropriately to a candidate's level of capabilities in emergency care, in the radio room and as a member of the crew (i.e., the candidate must not be overeager to prove himself and thus interfere with a call or be disrespectful to the members and advisers of the post).

16. Candidate maintains at least a "C" or 2.0 average in school.

17. Candidate displays interest and enthusiasm for upgrading his/her level of EMS qualifications and skills through participation in discussions and training sessions.

18. Candidate learns to be self-confident and self-reliant when performing a responsibility independently.

19. Candidate functions well under stress and demonstrates that he/she thinks before acting.

20. Candidate receives constructive criticism well, and responds quickly and willingly to that given by an adviser or member.

21. Candidate demonstrates enthusiasm and sincerity in becoming a member of Post 53.

Candidate's Signature Signature of Parent/Guardian

Sponsor's Signature

THE ROLE OF A SPONSOR

1. The Sponsor is responsible for clarifying the responsibility involved with the post, and the attitude the candidate must have toward all the members.

2. The Sponsor should sit down with his/her candidate every two weeks and discuss the candidate checklist and how well the candidate is fulfilling the requirements of the checklist. Sponsor should have five members every two weeks fill out the candidate checklist concerning his/her candidate and discuss these results with the candidate.

3. The Sponsor must attend the officers meeting every three weeks and discuss the candidate with the officers. The Sponsor should be prepared to discuss how the membership feels about the candidate.

4. If the Sponsor receives a compliment or complaint about the candidate, he/she must go to that person and have him/her fill out the candidate checklist.

5. It is the Sponsor's job to make sure the candidate grows and matures with knowledge.

6. The Sponsor should be aware of any problems concerning the candidate at all times. This includes questioning the membership.

7. The Sponsor must be a *motivator!* A Sponsor cannot be afraid to be stern with a candidate for fear that he/she may be intimidated.

8. It is the responsibility of the membership to shape motivated, hard-working candidates. Lately we have had a tendency to be easy on candidates on voting night. This will only hurt the post and all the postees. Not only the Sponsor but also the entire membership must play an active role in shaping a good candidate. We must set our expectations of the candidate at the highest level.

Sample Parental Release, Medical and Vaccination Forms

PARENTAL RELEASE FORM

This is to certify that I/we have read and understand all facets of the Membership Assistance Program and the Health Program of Explorer Post #53–Darien Emergency Medical Services as set forth in the bylaws and operations procedures of that organization. It is also understood that all adults and members of minor age are required to follow these rules in order to retain membership.

I/We give permission for (print)_____, our minor child, to participate in all aspects of the bylaws and operations procedures as set forth in that document dated April 1991.

Print   _____

          Name   Address   Relationship

Signature _____

Date   _____

Print   _____

          Name   Address   Relationship

Signature _____

Date   _____

MEDICAL FORM

(To be filled in and signed by family doctor)

All rider trainees must have this form completed to ride the ambulance.

Applicant's Name _____

Blood pressure _____ Pulse _____ Vision (Corrected) _____

Has the applicant ever suffered any illness/injury that might be aggravated by the strenuous demands of activities in an ambulance corps? _____
If yes, explain:

_____

_____

_____

Does the applicant show evidence of any physical condition that would prevent loading stretchers (i.e., back problems)?

_____

_____

Does the applicant show evidence of any physical condition which would interfere with the safe operation of an emergency vehicle? _____
If yes, explain:

_____

_____

_____

Does the applicant currently take any medications?_____
If yes, explain:

_____

Overall evaluation of the applicant's condition for membership in Darien Emergency Medical Services:_____

I have examined the above-named applicant and hereby certify that to the best of my knowledge he/she is free from any physical medical or mental condition that might prevent performance of duties as a member of Darien Emergency Medical Services:

Date _____ Signature _____

Address _____

HEPATITIS B VIRUS VACCINE CONSENT OR REFUSAL FORM FOR:

_____

Print name

CONSENT FOR THE USE OF HEPATITIS B VIRUS VACCINE

I have received and read a copy of the pamphlet entitled "Hepatitis B: A Disease in the Need of Prevention" or viewed the "Preventing Hepatitis B: The Vaccination Decision" videotape (prepared by MSD, 1990) and had all my questions answered to my satisfaction. I understand the Pharmaceutical Manufacturer's Administration dosage and time schedule. I understand that in order for the Hepatitis B vaccine to be fully effective, I must complete the Pharmaceutical Manufacturer's Administration dosage and time schedule. I understand that most recipients develop immunity to Hepatitis B, but some (10%) of the recipients fail to develop Hepatitis B surface antibody. I also understand that the vaccine will not protect me from Hepatitis A or non-A, non-B Hepatitis, but, if successful, will protect me from Hepatitis D (Delta). The material risks of the Hepatitis B virus vaccine have been explained to me. I agree to receive the Hepatitis B vaccine.

Signature: _____ Date: _____

Parent or Guardian if under the age of eighteen: _____

Witness: _____ Date: _____

REFUSAL FOR THE USE OF HEPATITIS B VIRUS VACCINE

I understand that due to my occupational exposure to blood or other potentially infectious materials, I may be at risk of acquiring Hepatitis B virus (HBV) infection. I have read a copy of the pamphlet entitled "Hepatitis B: A Disease in the Need of Prevention" or viewed the "Preventing Hepatitis B: The Vaccination Decision" videotape (prepared by MSD, 1990) and had all my questions answered to my satisfaction. I understand that by declining this vaccine, I continue to be at risk of acquiring Hepatitis B, a potentially life-threatening disease. If, in the future, I continue to operate in the environment, and choose to be vaccinated with the Hepatitis B vaccine, I can receive the vaccination series at no charge to me. At this time I decline the Hepatitis B vaccine.

Signature: _____ Date: _____

Parent or Guardian if under the age of eighteen: _____

Witness: _____ Date: _____

GLOSSARY

Cardiac. A person with heart disease.

Cardiopulmonary resuscitation (CPR). The technique of restoring heartbeat or breathing.

Certification. The state of having fulfilled the requirements needed to practice in a given field.

Chlorine. A heavy greenish yellow gas with a sharp odor.

Crisis. An unstable event or state of affairs whose outcome will make a difference for better or worse.

Evidence. Something that furnishes proof.

Extrication. The act of freeing someone from an entanglement or difficulty.

Forensic. Belonging to or used in courts of law.

Hepatitis. Inflammation of the liver.

Liability release form. A signed statement that relieves an organization from responsibility for damage or personal injury.

Polygraph. An instrument that records variations in pulse (i.e., lie detector).

Probation. Subjection to a period of testing and trial to determine fitness for a job or for school.

Robert's Rules of Order. An internationally accepted rule book on procedures in conducting a meeting.

Scut work. Work that is ordinary, basic, uninspiring but has to be done, often as the foundation for more important work.

Urinalysis. Chemical analysis of urine.

Verbatim transcript. Word-for-word, recorded exactly as the speaker said it.

BIBLIOGRAPHY

Arco Editorial Board. *Allied Health Professions.* New York: Prentice Hall, 1993.

"Bylaws and Operational Procedures." Darien, CT: Explorer Post 53, Darien Emergency Medical Services, 1996.

"Cadet Program: Setting the Pace for Tomorrow's Leaders." Maxwell Air Force Base, AL: Civil Air Patrol (undated).

Casagrande, Kate. "Junior firefighters learn the ropes." *Voices,* Southbury, CT (March 5, 1997): 33.

"CPR." *The Encyclopedia Americana International Edition,* Vol. 8. Danbury, CT: Grolier, 1994.

"Darien Emergency Medical Services." Darien, CT: Explorer Post 53, Darien Emergency Medical Services (undated).

Detwiler, Eric. "Teens to the rescue: Explorer post responds to medical emergencies." *Stamford Advocate,* Stamford, CT (August 26, 1996).

Doebler, Moritz. "Explorers learn more than police work." *Danbury News-Times,* Danbury, CT (May 11, 1994): A1, A5.

"Emergency Medical Services." Fairfield, CT: Southwestern Connecticut Emergency Medical Services Council, Inc. (undated).

Everett, Melissa. "EMS wish list short." *The Wilton Bulletin,* Wilton, CT (January 29, 1997).

"Explorer Post 53 named a Point of Light by Bush." *The Hour.* Norwalk, CT (August 7, 1992).

Greenlees, Robert. "Teen Angels." *Heartland USA,* (Summer 1992).

Kovach, John. "DHS parents learn how Post 53 works." *Darien News-Review,* Darien, CT (October 12, 1995).

"Law Enforcement Explorer Manual." Danbury, CT: Law Enforcement Explorer Post 33, Danbury Police Department, 1994.

"Manual and By-Laws." Southbury, CT: Explorer Post 130, Southbury Police Department, 1995.

McGovern, Michael. "Post 53: 25 years of priceless service." *Darien News-Review,* Darien, CT (July 6, 1995): 3.

——————————. "New law could hurt Post 53." *Darien News-Review,* Darien, CT (December 12, 1996): A1, A15.

O'Neill, Laurie A. "Youths Run Town's Ambulance Service." *The New York Times* (May 26, 1996).

Royce, Lynn. "A Tale of Two Boys." *Danbury News-Times,* Danbury, CT (July 10, 1994).

"Scholarship Information for Scouts and Explorers." Irving, TX: Boy Scouts of America, 1995.

Silberlicht, Maria. "Will town foot bill for dedicated paramedics?" *Darien News-Review,* Darien, CT (November 22, 1995): A10.

"Teen volunteers honored for outstanding service." *Darien News-Review,* Darien, CT (April 28, 1994): 28.

Von Ohlsen, Sherry. "Teen medics save lives." *The World.* (December 1992): 408–415.

"What Do Aerospace Education, Emergency Services, and Cadet Programs have in Common?" Maxwell Air Force Base, AL: *Civil Air Patrol,* 1996.

SUGGESTIONS FOR FURTHER READING

Fletcher, Connie. *Pure Cop: Cop Talk from the Street to the Specialized Units—Bomb Squad, Arson, Hostage Negotiation, Prostitution, Major Accidents, Crime Scene.* New York: Villard Books, 1991.

——————————. *What Cops Know: Cops Talk about What They Do, How They Do It, and What It Does to Them.* New York: Villard Books, 1991.

Hays, Gayleen, with Kathleen Moloney. *Policewoman One: My Twenty Years on the LAPD.* New York: Villard Books, 1992.

McArdle, Phil, and Karen McArdle. *Fatal Fascination: Where Fact Meets Fiction in Police Work.* Boston: Houghton Mifflin, 1988.

Rachlin, Harvey. *The Making of a Cop.* New York: W.W. Norton, 1991.

——————————. *The Making of a Detective.* New York: Pocket Books, 1995.

Sparrow, Malcolm K., Mark H. Moore, and David M. Kennedy. *Beyond 911: A New Era for Policing.* New York: Basic Books (HarperCollins), 1990.

Thompson, George J., and Jerry B. Jenkins. *Verbal Judo: The Gentle Art of Persuasion.* New York: Morrow, 1993.

The following books may be in the Young Adult or Juvenile section of your library. Don't be put off because they are "children's books." They offer good photographs and descriptions with plenty of detail.

Blumberg, Rhoda. *Fire Fighters.* New York: Franklin Watts, 1976.

Da Costa, Phil. *100 Years of America's Fire-fighting Apparatus, 1873–1963.* New York: Bonanza Books, 1964.

Ingram, Arthur. *A History of Fire Fighting and Equipment.* Secaucus, NJ: Chartwell Books, 1978.

Reuter, Margaret. *Careers in a Fire Department.* Milwaukee: Raintree Publications Ltd.—Children's Press, 1977.

The following books will help give you a broad understanding of volunteerism and opportunities in community service.

Berkowitz, Bill. *Local Heroes: The Rebirth of Heroism in America.* Lexington, MA: Lexington Books (D.C. Heath), 1987.

Buckley, William F., Jr. *Gratitude: Reflections on What We Owe to Our Country.* New York: Random House, 1990.

Coles, Robert. *The Call of Service: A Witness to Idealism.* Boston: Houghton Mifflin, 1993.

Daloz, Laurent A., et al. *Common Fire: Lives of Commitment in a Complex World.* Boston: Beacon Press, 1996.

Griggs, John, editor. *Simple Acts of Kindness: Volunteering in the Age of AIDS.* New York: United Hospital Fund of New York, 1989.

Luks, Allan, with Peggy Payne. *The Healing Power of Doing Good: The Health and Spiritual Benefits of Helping Others.* New York: Fawcett Columbine, 1991.

Olasky, Marvin. *Renewing American Compassion.* New York: The Free Press (Simon & Schuster), 1996.

Tarshis, Lauren. *Taking Off: Extraordinary Ways to Spend Your First Year Out of College.* New York: Fireside (Simon & Schuster), 1989.

Wuthnow, Robert. *Acts of Compassion: Caring for Others and Helping Ourselves.* Princeton, NJ: Princeton University Press, 1991.